GRIMM'S
Hansel and Gretel

Illustrated by Antonella Bolliger-Savelli

OXFORD UNIVERSITY PRESS
NEW YORK

There was once a poor woodcutter and his wife who lived on the edge of a great forest with their two children, Hansel and Gretel. The woodcutter had nothing in the world he could call his own, and indeed he had scarcely bread enough for his wife and the two children to eat. At last the time came when even that was all gone, and he knew not where to seek for help.

Then at night, as he lay on his bed and turned himself here and there, restless and full of care, his wife said to him 'Husband, listen to me, and take the two children out early tomorrow morning; give each of them a piece of bread, and then lead them into the midst of the wood where it is thickest, make a fire for them, and go away and leave them alone to shift for themselves, for we can no longer keep them here.'

'No, wife,' said the husband, 'I cannot find it in my heart to leave the children to the wild beasts of the forest, who would soon tear them to pieces.'

'Well, if you will not do as I say,' answered the wife, 'we must all starve together:' and she let him have no peace until he agreed to her plan.

Meantime the poor children too were lying awake, restless and weak from hunger, so that they heard all that their mother said to her husband. Gretel began to weep. But Hansel crept to her bed-side, and said, 'Do not be afraid, Gretel, I will find some help for us.' Then he got up, put on his jacket, and opened the door and went out.

The moon shone bright upon the little court before the cottage, and the white pebbles glittered like daisies on the green meadows. So he stooped down, and put as many as he could into his pocket, and then went back to the house. 'Now, Gretel,' said he, 'rest in peace;' and he went to bed and fell fast asleep.

Early in the morning, before the sun had risen, the woodman's wife came and woke them. 'Get up, children,' said she, 'we are going into the wood; there is a piece of bread for each of you, but take care of it and keep some for the afternoon.'

Gretel took the bread and carried it in her apron, because Hansel had his pocket full of stones, and they made their way into the wood.

After they had walked on for a time, Hansel stood still and looked towards home, and after a while turned again, and so on several times. Then his father said, 'Hansel, why do you keep turning and lagging about so? Move your legs on a little faster.'

'Ah, Father,' answered Hansel, 'I am stopping to look at my white cat that sits on the roof, and wants to say good-bye to me.'

'You little fool,' said his mother, 'that is not your cat; 'tis the morning sun shining on the chimney-top.'

Now Hansel had not been looking at the cat, but had been staying behind to drop from his pocket one white pebble after another along the road.

When they came into the midst of the wood, the woodman said, 'Run about, children, and pick up some wood, and I will make a fire to keep us all warm.'

So they piled up a little heap of brushwood, and set it alight; and as the flames burnt bright, the mother said, 'Now sit yourselves by the fire and go to sleep, while we go and cut wood in the forest; be sure you wait till we come again and fetch you.'

Hansel and Gretel sat by the fireside till the afternoon, and then each of them ate their piece of bread. They fancied the woodman was still in the wood, because they thought they heard the blows of his axe; but it was a bough which he had cunningly hung upon a tree, so that the wind blew it backwards and forwards, and it sounded like the axe as it hit the other boughs. Thus they waited till evening; but the woodman and his wife kept away, and no one came to fetch them.

When it was quite dark Gretel began to cry; but Hansel said, 'Wait awhile till the moon rises.' And when the moon rose, he took her by the hand, and there lay the pebbles along the ground, glittering like new pieces of money, and marked the way out. Towards morning they came again to the woodman's house, and he was glad in his heart when he saw the children again; for he had grieved at leaving them alone. His wife also seemed to be glad; but in her heart she was angry at it.

Not long after there was again no bread in the house, and Hansel and Gretel heard the wife say to her husband, 'The children found their way back once, and I took it in good part; but there is only half a loaf of bread left for them in the house; tomorrow we must take them deeper into the wood, that they may not find their way out, or we shall all be starved.'

It grieved the husband in his heart to do as his wife wished, and he thought it would be better to share their last morsel with the children; but as he had done as she said once, he did not dare to say no.

When the children heard their plan, Hansel got up and wanted to pick up pebbles as before; but when he came to the door he found his mother had locked it.

Early in the morning a piece of bread was given to each of them, but still smaller than the one they had before. Upon the road Hansel crumbled his in his pocket, and often stood still, and threw a crumb upon the ground.

'Why do you lag behind so, Hansel?' said the woodman. 'Walk in front with Gretel.'

'I am looking at my little dove that is sitting upon the roof.'

'You silly boy,' said the wife, 'that is not your little dove, it is the morning sun that shines on the chimney-top.'

But Hansel went on crumbling his bread, and throwing it on the ground. And thus they went on still further into the wood, where they had never been before in all their life.

There they were again told to sit down by a large fire, and sleep; and the woodman and his wife said they would come in the evening and fetch them away. In the afternoon Hansel shared Gretel's bread, because he had strewed all his upon the road; but the day passed away, and evening passed away too, and no one came to the poor children. Still Hansel comforted Gretel, and said, 'Wait till the moon rises; then I shall see the crumbs of bread which I have strewed, and they will show us the way home.'

The moon rose; but when Hansel looked for the crumbs they were gone; for thousands of little birds in the wood had found them and picked them up. Hansel, however, set out to try and find his way home; but they soon lost themselves in the wilderness, and went on through the night and all the next day, till at last they lay down and fell asleep for weariness: and another day they went on as before, but still did not reach the end of the wood, and were as hungry as could be, for they had nothing to eat.

In the afternoon of the third day they came to a strange little hut, made of bread, with a roof of cake, and windows of sparkling sugar.

'Now we will sit down and eat till we have had enough,' said Hansel; 'I will eat off the roof for my share; you eat the windows, Gretel, they will be nice and sweet for you.'

Whilst Gretel, however, was picking at the sugar, a sweet pretty voice called from within:

> 'Tip, tap, who goes there?'

But the children answered:

> 'The wind, the wind,
> That blows through the air'

and went on eating.

Gretel had just broken out a round pane of the window for herself, and Hansel had just torn off a large piece of cake from the roof, when the door opened, and a little old lady came hobbling out. At this Gretel and Hansel were so frightened that they let fall what they had in their hands.

But the old lady shook her head, and said, 'Dear children, where have you been wandering about? Come in with me; you shall have something good.'

So she took them both by the hand, and led them into her little hut, and brought out plenty to eat—milk and pancakes, with sugar, apples, and nuts; and then two beautiful little beds were got ready, and Hansel and Gretel laid themselves down, and thought they were in Heaven: but the old lady was a spiteful one, and had made her pretty sweetmeat house to entrap little children.

Early in the morning, before they were awake, she went to their little beds, and when she saw the two sleeping so sweetly, she had no pity on them, but was glad they were in her power. Then she took up Hansel, and put him in a little cage by himself; and when he awoke, he found himself behind a grating, shut up as little chickens are: but she shook Gretel, and called out, 'Get up, you lazy thing, and fetch some water; and go into the kitchen and cook something good to eat: your brother is shut up yonder; I shall first fatten him, and when he is fat, I think I shall eat him.'

Gretel began to weep, but her tears were in vain, for she had to obey the witch. Every day the witch gave Hansel all kinds of good things to eat, but to Gretel she gave only the scraps. Each morning the old woman would hobble up to Hansel's cage and croak: 'Hansel, stick out your finger, so that I may feel how fat you are growing.' But Hansel stuck an old bone through the bars, and the old witch, whose eyes were dim, thought it was Hansel's finger, and wondered why he was not growing fatter.

After four weeks, when Hansel was still as thin as before, she lost patience, and said she would wait no longer. 'Come on, Gretel,' she called, 'hurry and fetch me some water. Whether or not Hansel is fat enough, tomorrow I am going to have my meal.'

Gretel was terrified at these words. 'If only the wild beasts of the forest had eaten us both together,' she said to herself, 'even that would have been better than this.'

Next morning Gretel had to get up early, light the fire, and hang a kettle of water above it to boil. 'But first we will bake some bread,' said the old witch. 'I have already heated the oven, and made the dough.'

She pushed poor Gretel outside to the oven, where the flames were already blazing. 'Climb inside,' said the witch, 'and see if it is hot enough for the dough to bake.'

Once Gretel was inside, the witch was going to shut her in to bake her with the bread. But Gretel saw what the witch had in mind, and said: 'How can I climb inside the oven? The door is too small.'

'Silly goose, of course it is big enough,' said the witch, 'look, even I can get inside.' And she stuck her head into the oven.

Then Gretel quickly pushed the witch right inside, slammed the oven-door shut, and bolted it fast. Well might the old witch howl now, but Gretel ran away, and the wicked old witch was left to burn.

Gretel ran straight to Hansel's cage, opened it, and cried with joy: 'Hansel! We are free at last! The witch is dead!'

Hansel leaped out of his cage, and how happy they were, the two of them! As they now had no need to be afraid, they went into the witch's house and filled all their pockets with jewels and good things to eat.

'But now we must go,' said Hansel, 'and escape from this forest before nightfall.'

After walking for some time they began to recognize their way, and at last they saw their father's house in the distance. Then they began to run.

And when they arrived at the door they kissed their father with joy at seeing him again.

The woodcutter had been very unhappy ever since he had left the children alone in the wood, and his wife was now dead.

Gretel shook all the jewels out of her apron, and there were enough there for all of them to live happily ever after.

Published in the United States by Oxford University Press,
200 Madison Avenue, New York, 1981

Published in Great Britain by Kaye & Ward Ltd,
Century House, 82–84 Tanner Street, London SE1 3PP, 1981

Text reprinted from Grimm's Fairy Tales (1962 edition) by
permission of Oxford University Press
Illustrations copyright © 1981 Kaye & Ward

British Library Cataloguing in Publication Data

Grimm, Jacob
    Hansel and Gretel.
    I. Title   II. Grimm, Wilhelm
    III. Bolliger-Savelli, Antonella
    398.2'1'0943   PZ8.1

ISBN 0-19-520262-7
Library of Congress Catalog Card Number 80-85054 (USA)

Printed in Great Britain by Hunter-James/Impact Litho. (Woking) Ltd.